D1305074

GETTING INTO NATURE™

GETTING INTO NATURE™

Owls

INSIDE AND OUT

Text by Gillian Houghton
Illustrations by Studio Stalio

The Rosen Publishing Group's
PowerKids Press™
New York

Published in 2004 in North America
by The Rosen Publishing Group, Inc.
29 East 21st Street, New York, NY 10010

Copyright © 2004
by Andrea Dué s.r.l., Florence, Italy, and
Rosen Book Works, Inc., New York, USA

First Edition

Book Design:
Andrea Dué s.r.l., Florence, Italy

Illustrations:
Studio Stalio (Ivan Stalio, Alessandro Cantucci, Fabiano Fabbrucci)
Map by Alessandro Bartolozzi

Library of Congress Cataloging-in-Publication Data
Houghton, Gillian.
Owls inside and out / Gillian Houghton.
   p. cm. — (Getting into nature)
Summary: Describes the physical characteristics of owls, where various
species can be found, their behavior, and myths about them.
Includes bibliographical references (p.   ).
ISBN 0-8239-4208-2 (lib. bdg.)
1. Owls—Juvenile literature. [1. Owls.] I. Title. II. Series.
QL696.S8H68 2004
598.9'7—dc22
                                                            2003015521

Manufactured in Italy by Eurolitho S.p.A., Milan

Contents

The Owl's Body

The owl has a head, an abdomen, or stomach area, two wings, and two feet. The owl's body is covered with a thick coat of soft feathers. These feathers form a pattern of brown, black, gray, and white, which allows the owl to be camouflaged, or hidden in its surroundings.

Compared to most North American birds, the owl has a very large head and brain. Its eyes are on the front of its head rather than the sides. The owl has a large feathered face, which is often crowned with large "horns" or "ears." These tufts of feathers are neither horns nor ears. The owl's real ears are hidden under feathers on either side of its face.

The owl has two large round eyes that are usually orange, yellow, or dark brown. Feathers spread up from the eyes like human eyebrows. The owl has a short, curved beak, which is a very sharp bill. The beak is sometimes hidden by whisker-like feathers.

Eagle owl
(*Bubo bubo*)

A Look Inside

The owl is a vertebrate, meaning that it has a skeleton, or frame of bones, to guard its insides. As in most birds, the owl's skeleton is light, which allows it to fly so well. A cranium, or skull, guards the owl's brain and is connected to the vertebrae of the neck. Vertebrae are the bony parts of the spine. These vertebrae are bendable enough to allow the owl to turn its head almost 180 degrees in either direction. It can see almost directly over its shoulder.

lungs ——

liver ——

intestines ——

In the owl's chest, the ribs and the sternum, or breastbone, guard the **organs** that make up the **respiratory**, **circulatory**, **digestive**, and **reproductive** systems. The large wing bones connect to small, fingerlike bones at the tips of the wings. The large leg bones connect to the claws. The claws are made up of small bones joined together, like those in human hands and feet.

wing feathers –

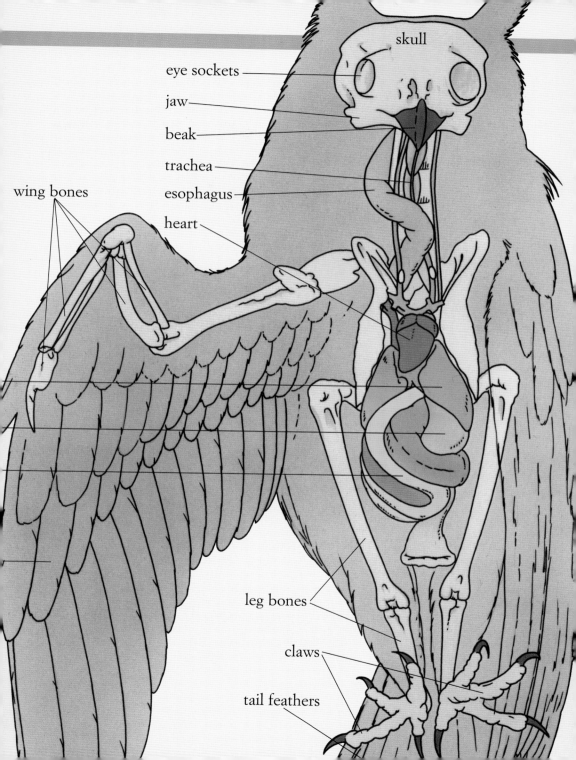

skull

eye sockets

jaw

beak

trachea

esophagus

heart

wing bones

leg bones

claws

tail feathers

The Owl's Range

Eagle owl
(*Bubo bubo*)

Little owl
(*Athene noctua*)

Some owls tend to be reclusive, meaning they like to live far away from human settlements. The great gray owl lives in oak forests. The elf owl lives in the saguaro cacti of the desert. The snowy owl lives in the arctic tundra, and the short-eared owl lives in prairies or marshes. The great horned owl can live in a wide range of surroundings. The western United States is home to the greatest number of different owl groups. Unlike most North American birds that travel south in the winter and north in the summer, the owl usually stays in one place all

Top left: The great horned owl is native to North, Central, and South America.

Right: The barred owl is native to North America.

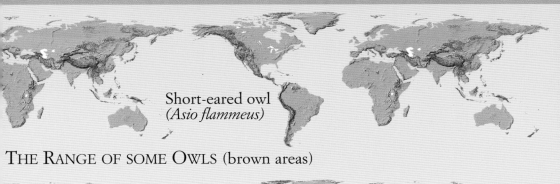

Short-eared owl
(*Asio flammeus*)

THE RANGE OF SOME OWLS (brown areas)

Barn owl
(*Tyto alba*)

year round. The owl will look for a new home only if it is having trouble finding food. Many owls are **nocturnal**, meaning they hunt mainly at night. Others like to hunt in the early morning and evening. Still others are **diurnal**, meaning they hunt during the day.

Below:
The barn owl is found on all continents.

Eyesight and Hearing

The owl has very good eyesight, which is necessary when hunting in dim light over a large piece of land. The owl has very large eyes, allowing it to see its surroundings very clearly. The eyes are shaped by bony plates called scleral ossicles, which are joined to the skull. These plates form a firm tube around the eye.

Whatever light is available is directed through this tube, allowing the owl to see clearly even in low light. When hunting, the owl may bob its head up and down or from side to side. This allows the owl to see its **prey** from several angles, giving it a better sense of the prey's exact location. The owl is also able to twist its neck so that its head appears upside-down and its eyes look directly up. This allows the owl to see objects above its usual sight lines.

Right: This is a drawing of the owl's eye and a chart of the owl's range of sight, which is 110 degrees total. Owls have 70 degree binocular vision, which is when both eyes see an object at once.

Below: This drawing shows how the ear openings of a tawny owl are set at different places on the skull. This unevenness allows the bird to figure out the direction and distance of a sound.

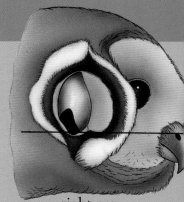

right ear

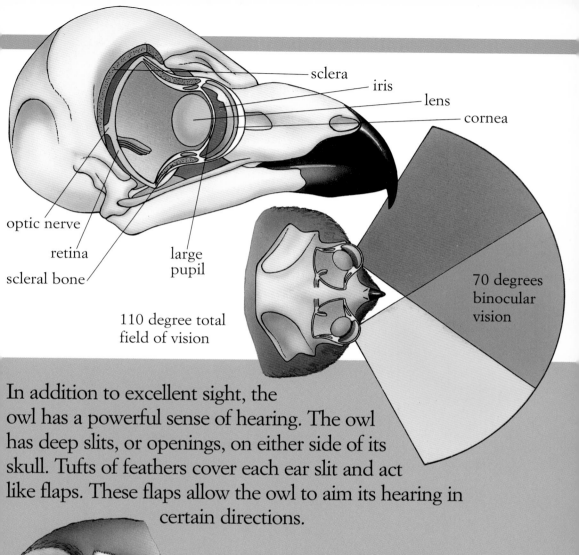

sclera

iris

lens

cornea

optic nerve

retina

large pupil

scleral bone

70 degrees binocular vision

110 degree total field of vision

In addition to excellent sight, the owl has a powerful sense of hearing. The owl has deep slits, or openings, on either side of its skull. Tufts of feathers cover each ear slit and act like flaps. These flaps allow the owl to aim its hearing in certain directions.

The owl's large head also plays a part in hearing. A sound will be received by one of the owl's ears before it reaches the other, allowing the owl to learn from what direction the sound is coming.

left ear

The Owl Family

Owls are some of the oldest **species** of birds on the planet. By studying **fossils**, scientists have learned that owls came into being some 70 million years ago. Around that time, the owl's **ancestors** began growing certain features, such as pointed and cutting claws and sharp eyesight, that made them master hunters. Over time, these features were perfected, while other features less important to their daily life were lost. This growth is called **evolution**. These first **primitive** owls grew into today's owls.

Short-eared owl (*Asio flammeus*)

Little owl (*Athene noctua*)

Snowy owl (*Nyctea scandiaca*)

Great gray owl
(*Strix nebulosa*)

Northern hawk owl
(*Surnia ulula*)

Spectacled owl
(*Pulsatrix
perspicillata*)

Barn owl
(*Tyto alba*)

Great
horned
owl (*Bubo
virginianus*)

13

The Owl's Beak and Claws

The owl's beak is shaped like a flattened hook. The sharp cutting beak is ideal for giving a deadly bite. Because it is narrow and points downward, the beak does not get in the way of the owl's field of sight.

The owl has two powerful claws, which have changed over millions of years to make the bird a deadly hunter. Each claw is made up of four toes. One toe spreads backward, while the other three face forward. Often the owl will turn the outer forward toe on each claw backward, so that two toes face forward and two face the rear. This gives the owl greater control and balance when sitting on a tree branch or seizing prey. Each toe has a talon, a sharp curved nail that can easily catch and tear prey. The claws are usually feathered to guard the owl from prey that may cut or bite when fighting back to escape danger.

Right: These are closeups of the head and claw of an eagle owl (*Bubo bubo*). Eagle owls are recognized by the two tufts of feathers above their bright orange eyes. They stand more than two feet tall (0.6 meters). Their sharp claws allow them to hunt rats, foxes, rabbits, birds, frogs, and fish.

The Capture of Prey

Owls fly silently through forests, deserts, lake areas, and even barns searching for prey. Smaller owls feed on insects and tiny animals, such as mice. Larger owls might enjoy bigger animals, such as rabbits, and game birds, such as pheasants. The owl is fairly light, and its wings are wide. These features allow it to fly and drift silently so that it does not scare away prey.

Below:
A male great gray owl (Strix nebulosa) brings a captured mouse to his family.

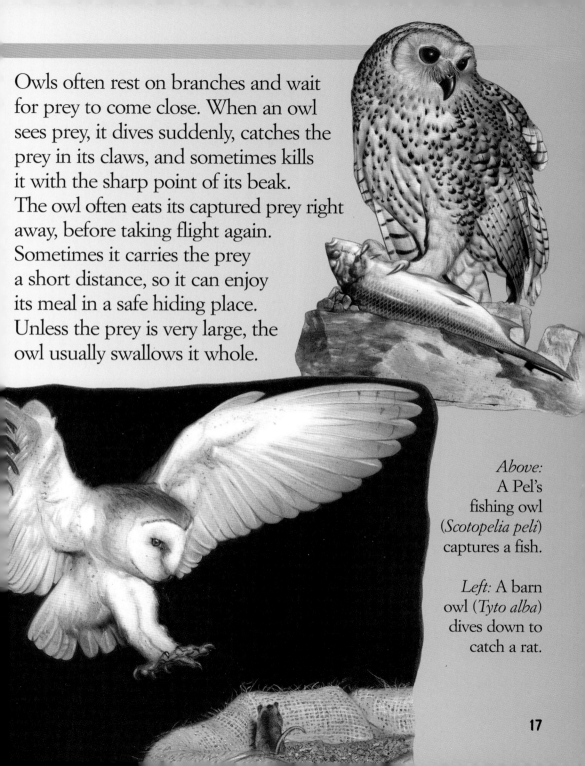

Owls often rest on branches and wait for prey to come close. When an owl sees prey, it dives suddenly, catches the prey in its claws, and sometimes kills it with the sharp point of its beak. The owl often eats its captured prey right away, before taking flight again. Sometimes it carries the prey a short distance, so it can enjoy its meal in a safe hiding place. Unless the prey is very large, the owl usually swallows it whole.

Above: A Pel's fishing owl (*Scotopelia peli*) captures a fish.

Left: A barn owl (*Tyto alba*) dives down to catch a rat.

Owl Pellets

Owls spit up solid waste known as pellets. They are small, firm, and oval in shape. Pellets are made up of matter—such as feathers, fur, and bones—that the owl eats during feeding but its stomach can not break down. Once this matter is packed together into a pellet, it rises up out of the stomach into the owl's mouth. On average, the owl **regurgitates**, or spits out of its mouth, two pellets per day. Pellets do not rot, or break down, very quickly. Therefore, the ground beneath an owl roost might be littered with pellets that are several years old.

Scientists collect and study these pellets to learn what kind of food an owl has eaten. This gives them knowledge about owl habits and the condition of the surroundings in which they live.

Below, left:
A Pel's fishing owl (*Scotopelia peli*) prepares to eat a fish it has just captured in Botswana, Africa.

Right:
A small skull and bones can be seen in this pellet left by a tawny owl (*Strix aluco*).

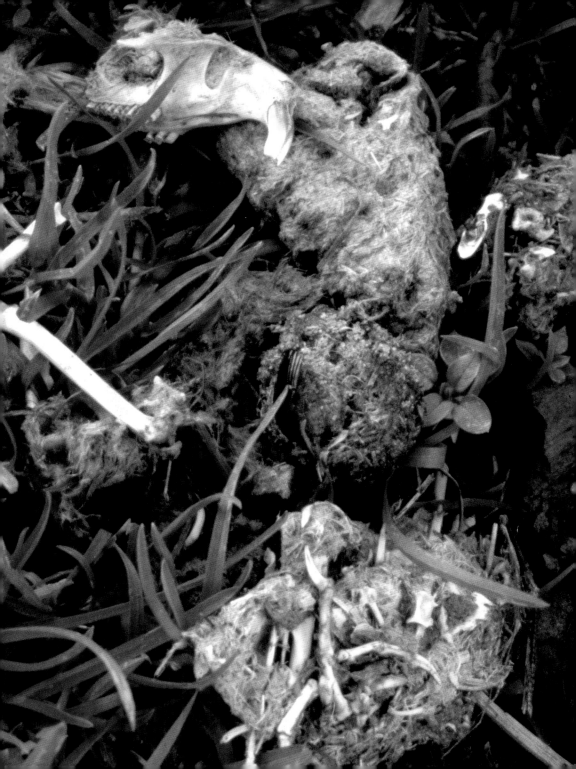

Mating and Laying Eggs

During the **breeding** season, a male, or boy, owl searches for a female, or girl, owl to become its **mate**. In the early evenings and into the night, the male calls to the female with a "hoot" or "whar" sound. Sometimes the male shows off with displays of wing clapping and flying. The female answers with her own **mating** call and approaches the male.

The location and size of the nest the two will build depends on the species. Some owls, like the great horned owl, make their nests on the rocky edges of mountains. Other owl species nest in the high branches of trees. The great gray owl often makes its home in the deserted nest of a buzzard or eagle. The female lays an egg every two or three days and then stays in the nest to **incubate** them, or keep them warm with the heat of her body. During this time, the male owl brings her food. After about thirty days, the chicks begin to hatch, or break out of their eggs.

Opposite, bottom: These chicks of the short-eared owl (*Asio flammeus*) are all different sizes because the mother lays and hatches each egg separately.

Right: Barn owls
(*Tyto alba*) got their
name because they make
their nests in the straw
stored in barns.

Left: Great gray owl chicks (*Strix nebulosa*) grow in nests built in trees.

Raising the Young

The number of chicks born to owls is different from species to species and changes from year to year. One year, a great horned owl may raise one or two owlets. The following year, if more food is available, the same owl may raise six or more owlets. On average, the great gray owl raises a clutch, or group of owlets, that numbers between four and five each year.

The chicks will remain in the nest for about three weeks before their first trip onto the branches of the tree or edge of the rock face where they were born. They must learn to fly and hunt for food. The clutch will stay in the neighborhood of the nest for several more months. Their mother will continue to look after them, while the father hunts for food for the family. When the male owl returns with large prey, the female will rip the prey apart into small pieces and feed it to her young.

Right: An eagle owl (*Bubo bubo*) family rests comfortably in its nest. Behind the mother and her chick, the father, half-hidden by branches, stands guard.

Right: A young little owl (*Athene noctua*) stares at a dung beetle before seizing and eating it.

Owl Tales

Many people believe that an owl's hoot is a sign of bad luck. The owl is also known and respected, however, for its wisdom, strength, and knowledge. It is not surprising that the owl fills us with a mix of fear and respect. The owl is a skilled hunter and often flies only in the dark of night. These habits add to its bad name. Yet the owl has an upright body position, a broad face, and large blinking eyes, as do humans. Because of this, humans give owls certain human features, such as cleverness.

These beliefs about the owl are not new. A Sumerian tablet dating from around 2300 BC shows the goddess of death, Lilith, surrounded by owls. In ancient Greece, the goddess of wisdom, Athena, was often pictured with a small owl. Greek myths, or tales, tell about soldiers who carried live owls into battle with them, giving them greater bravery in war.

Today, in books, cartoons, and TV ads, our ancient curiosity about the owl lives on.

Opposite, top: The ancient Greeks often associated owls with wisdom and strength in battle. As a result, the owl appears on many Greek artifacts. One of these is the seventh century BC owl-shaped vessel pictured here.

Opposite, bottom: A Greek vase painting of the fourth century BC shows an owl dressed in the goddess Athena's armor.

Top, right: Ancient Athenian coins often pictured the owl, a sign of Athena, the goddess of wisdom, and of Athens, the city named for her.

Bottom, right: The belief that owls are wise continues today, as seen in this modern cartoon.

Glossary

ancestors (AN-ses-ters) The older or earlier plants and animals to which modern plants and animals are related.

breeding (BREED-ing) The act of making babies.

circulatory (SUR-kyuh-luh-tor-ee) Relating to the flow of blood throughout the body.

digestive (die-JES-tiv) Relating to the breaking down of food.

diurnal (die-UR-nul) A creature that is active in the daytime.

evolution (eh-vuh-LOO-shun) The gradual changes that plants and animals undergo over many years.

fossils (FAH-suls) Traces of plants or animals preserved in the Earth's crust.

incubate (IN-kyoo-bayt) To sit on eggs and warm them until they hatch.

mate (MAYT) To join together two bodies in order to make babies.

mating (MAYT-ing) Relating to the joining together of two bodies in order to make babies.

nocturnal (nok-TUR-nul) A creature that is active at night.

organs (OR-gunz) Groups of cells or body parts that have specific jobs to perform in the body.

prey (PRAY) An animal hunted and killed by another animal for food.

primitive (PRIH-muh-tiv) Similar to one's earliest ancestors. Something in a very early stage of development.

regurgitates (re-GUR-juh-taytz) Brings food back up to the mouth from the stomach.

reproductive (re-pruh-DUK-tiv) Relating to the making of babies.

respiratory (RES-puh-ruh-tor-ee) Relating to the act of breathing.

species (SPEE-shees) A group of plants or animals that have similar physical characteristics.

Index

Web Sites

Due to the changing nature of Internet links, PowerKids Press has developed an online list of Web sites related to the subject of this book. This site is updated regularly. Please use this link to access the list:

www.powerkidslinks.com/gin/owl

About the Author

Gillian Houghton is an editor and freelance writer in New York City.

Photo Credits